Paul & Mat

AVOIDING THE PITFALLS OF FAMILIARITY

Mark T. Barclay

All scripture references are quoted from the
King James Version of the Holy Bible
unless otherwise noted.

Second Edition
First Printing 1997

ISBN 0-944802-29-X

Published by: Mark Barclay Ministries
aka Mark Barclay Publications

Printed in USA

Write:
Mark Barclay Ministries
P.O. Box 588, Midland, MI 48640-0588

CONTENTS

Chapter 1 — Jesus Faced It 1

Chapter 2 — The "Equalizers" 5

Chapter 3 — The Art of Dissension 11

Chapter 4 — Aborting Miracles 19

Chapter 5 — The Name of a Prophet 21

Chapter 6 — The Three Zones of Life 27

Chapter 7 — Life's Examples 33

Chapter 8 — Bible Examples 43

Chapter 9 — Local Church Examples 51

Chapter 10 — Fighting the Sin 55

Prayer of Salvation

CHAPTER 1
JESUS FACED IT

"And it came to pass, that when Jesus had finished these parables, he departed thence.

And when he was come into his own country, he taught them in their synagogue, insomuch that they were astonished, and said, Whence hath this man this wisdom, and these mighty works?

Is not this the carpenter's son? is not his mother called Mary? and his brethren, James, and Joses, and Simon, and Judas?

And his sisters, are they not all with us? Whence then hath this man all these things?

And they were offended in him. But Jesus said unto them, A prophet is not without honour, save in his own country, and in his own house.

And he did not many mighty works there because of their unbelief."

Matthew 13:53-58

PREACHING THAT ASTOUNDS

Jesus was, and still is, the greatest preacher and teacher of all time. He taught in such a way that people would comment on His authority. He could cause disciples to reason among themselves. In one parable, Jesus would feed His flock and rebuke His foes. One word from this divine orator's mouth could raise the dead and condemn the wicked. What a treat to walk in His steps and study His life!

In Matthew 13:53-58, which we are using as our text, we see that this marvelous teacher had come to the city of Nazareth to teach in their synagogue. Now keep in mind that Jesus, to the people in this passage of scripture, was not yet recognized to be the resurrected Lord and Savior as we know Him today. No, quite the contrary. These Nazarenes didn't even receive Him as a qualified teacher of His time.

Even so, we find this preacher, Jesus, teaching in their synagogue. He was like a traveling speaker to them, a guest, one who had come into their church service to share the things of the Kingdom.

You and I both know that it didn't take Jesus long at all to get their full attention. Even though He was just another preacher to them, He was the Master. They hadn't heard anyone teach quite like this before.

As He spoke to them, they became astonished at His words. They were sitting on the edge of their seats. They were listening with great interest and a thrill in their hearts.

He began to testify of all the works of God that were being done in His ministry. He began to tell them the revelation of Heaven. The number one oracle of Heaven was in their midst, and they didn't even know it, yet they were astonished at His words.

This is the way it is supposed to be. People who are hearing from Heaven should marvel at Heaven's words. We should never get used to Heaven's miracles or the works of Christ in our midst.

Nazareth was being visited by the greatest of all visitors. The congregation of this synagogue had a chance of a lifetime. These people were attending the greatest church service ever to be held in their city!

THE FIRST STATEMENT

A Statement of Respect and Reception

Matthew 13:54 reveals to us the conflict between truth and error, humility and pride, Heaven and earth, the preacher and the listener, and the leadership and the congregation. The sin of all sins was about to be revealed!

First of all, listen to the statement that was made that day in the synagogue of Nazareth as Jesus spoke:

> *". . . Where did this man get this wisdom and these miraculous powers? . . . "*
>
> Matthew 13:54 (NIV)

They were commenting on His wisdom. They were amazed at His power. They were astonished. I know people like this. They come into a church, and they marvel at the work. They speak flattering things, and they speak of the blessings and the hand of the Lord upon you. They listen to the wisdom of, and they enjoy the presence of, the powerful Holy Spirit. They sound and look like characters taken right out of this Nazareth synagogue.

Their hunger gets stirred up (among other things), and

they immediately wonder why they aren't like the pastor. They wonder why their ministry isn't flourishing in the same way. They soon begin to harbor the wrong thoughts—and those thoughts lead them to *do wrong things*!

CHAPTER 2
THE "EQUALIZERS"

Did you know that every local church congregation has an "equalizer"? Well, they do. These are the people who speak up and stand against leadership in order to defame them. They are always questioning the pastor and trying to take away the esteem that he may have in the hearts of the flock. They work hard and scheme to make God's ordained leader equal (in authority) to everyone else. They try to make him their peer rather than their leader.

Why are there people like this? It's the devil's way of uprooting sheep and leading them to slaughter. It's his way of scattering the sheep, by means of dissension and strife. Harm the shepherd—scatter the sheep.

Why would anyone who claims to be a Christian want to be involved in such a thing? Jealousy and envy lead them to "equalize" the leader and draw disciples after themselves. They don't realize that no one has ever gotten away with this. God makes sure that they don't!

Here in Matthew 13:55-56, the equalizers even showed up at Jesus' meetings. Right in the midst of a divine display of power and wisdom, these equalizers began to form doubts and questions. They immediately went to work.

All of you preachers and teachers, listen to me. If they were bold enough to do this right to Jesus' face, don't think for a minute that we can escape it. If this attitude broke out in *His* church services, then it will break out in ours too. If they questioned *His* words and works with suspicion, then there will be some who question ours too. If it hindered the power flow of Jesus, it will have an influence on ours also.

Look at what they said here in Matthew 13:55-56:

"Is not this the carpenter's son? is not his mother called Mary? and his brethren, James, and Joses, and Simon, and Judas?

And his sisters, are they not all with us? Whence then hath this man all these things?"

These statements, made by the equalizers, made no real sense at all. There was no intelligence in them. They were not even questioning doctrine or lifestyle. They were simply trying to make Jesus equal to themselves. They were trying to lower His platform of authority in everyone else's eyes. This is the shame of questioning, doubting, and suspicious people. They always have to ruin things for everyone else. They are never satisfied to sin alone.

This technique is ages old. The equalizers are looking for anything they can use to *become familiar with Jesus*. I don't mean this in a good way. They were asking questions that would seed in the minds of others that this preacher was no different than anyone else. They wanted everyone to feel extra "comfy" around Him. You know: "Let your hair down." "He's no different than the rest of us." "He puts His pants on just like we do." "He has no special ministry." "Does the Lord speak only through Him?"

I hope that you can see it. I hope that you can see that

most people who ask questions like these are not hungry but rather antagonistic. They are breeding doubt and unbelief.

THE SIN OF FAMILIARITY

I've been asking congregations all over this country what they think the number one sin is. I get a tremendous amount of response and variety, but I have never yet had anyone answer—the sin of familiarity. That's right! It is by far the deadliest, yet subtlest, sin of all. It is like a slow, aging death. It is killing our children, ruining our marriages, defaming our preachers, splitting our churches, and defiling us in many other ways—daily! I will explain this better later on in this book.

In verse 56, we can see how these people (equalizers) had drawn their own conclusions. They had asked enough questions that they now had doubt in operation. They had determined that Jesus was not anointed. He was nothing special. He was no different than they were. He was not one of divine authority. They concluded, "Why should we listen to Him or be led by Him?"

". . . Where then did this man get all these things?"

Matthew 13:56 (NIV)

"Where then?" "Where then?" Can you see it? They had drawn their own conclusions (by questioning and "equalizing") that Jesus did not get His sermons from Heaven and that this power and these mighty works must be of some other origin. What a shame!

Listen, friends, churches are filled with people like this. I could write a whole book just about the people who have tried to do this in my ministry. I won't, but I could.

THE MODERN-DAY "EQUALIZERS"

These modern-day equalizers do and say the same things that their forerunners did and said. They nitpick and quibble over the pettiest stuff. They strain at a gnat and swallow a camel.

They say things like, "He's just a man like we are. He puts his britches on just like we do. Who does he think he is talking to us like that? What right does he have, confronting us this way? This is a one-man show. I think there's something funny going on with the money here."

It's like "Pop, Goes the Weasel," only I call these people equalizers instead of weasels. An equalizer is one who wants to strip or rape someone of all of their authority, esteem, and position of favor. They want to equalize all authority. They want to put a stop to a leader influencing his following. Every church today has them. Every business has them.

The sheep of God's pasture want to come and be fed by God's shepherd. They hold their leaders in high esteem. They respect God's men. They look up to them and desire to follow their leadership and direction, but there are plenty of people—equalizers—who will provide a few words of dissension and smut in order to demoralize the pastor in the middle of his congregation. They somehow think they are the antidote.

These equalizers are whisperers. They make midnight phone calls and have private, smutty meetings—all in the name of good. They minister at the front door of church buildings with gossip, slander, and talebearing techniques. They know their job very well.

These people will use the silliest words to defame and to cripple the reputations of God's leaders. What a ministry! What a call in life—to sow discord among the brethren and pollute the Kingdom with nastiness. What a shame! *Watch out for these people*—they just might be your relatives or your closest friends!

FROM ASTONISHED TO OFFENDED

Can you believe it? Before Jesus was finished teaching that day, people were offended. They went from astonished to offended in one sitting. It seems impossible, but it certainly isn't.

They were offended by Him. These people talked among themselves until they were convinced that Jesus did not get His wisdom and power from above. Look at verse 56:

> *". . . Where then did this man get all these things?"*

"Where then?" "Where then?" Listen, friend, this is the question of all questions. The following reasoning will get you in big trouble: Does my pastor hear from God or not? Did this sermon of his come from the Holy Spirit or not? Is he a gift of God to me or not? Where is he coming from? Where did he get this stuff? Where??????

Once you begin to question like this, you will begin to doubt. Once you begin to doubt, you will misunderstand your pastor's teachings and actions. As soon as you question and reason like this, you place yourself in jeopardy. You will find reason enough to offend and be offended.

You and I probably can't even imagine how the Lord Jesus could offend anyone, yet these people were offended.

I'm sure those who observed this whole thing spoke of how the people who got offended were good people, the faithful of the flock, the good givers, singers, prayer warriors, and attenders. Surely *they* wouldn't do anything that was wrong, *but* they did, *and* it still happens today!

These people went from being astonished to being offended. People today who equalize suffer the same thing. People who don't receive their leaders suffer the same thing.

CHAPTER 3
THE ART OF DISSENSION

Some people have made an art of causing dissension and division. They have made a job out of splitting churches and defaming pastors. Even some children have perfected the system of conniving their parents and performing wrongdoings and then giggle about it behind their parents' backs.

Do you know who you least want to receive correction from? Your subordinates. That's right! No one likes to take orders from the people who are under them in authority. Parents do not take orders from their children. The President of the United States doesn't take orders from his Cabinet members. The chairman of the board does not take direct orders from people under his authority, nor does the employer from the employee, nor does the pastor from the flock.

I realize that many people have a great problem with this. I realize that many people feel that this is unfair, unscriptural, and some kind of "shepherdship" error, but I tell you, my friend, it is not! It is more than proper to sit at someone's feet to learn. All of the great men and women of the Bible sat, at one time or another, at someone's feet to learn. Someone was their master teacher. They esteemed someone more highly than themselves.

There's an old rule. I say it like this: If you do not esteem someone more highly than yourself (someone you consider more important than yourself, someone whom you respect as much—if not more—than yourself, someone whose teaching and lifestyle you admire), then you will find yourself sitting at your own feet to learn. You will become your own teacher. That's dangerous because the next step is that you become your own advisor; then you become your own counselor.

The Bible states that only a fool thinks he's right in his own mind. It's of utmost importance that everyone, including leaders, has someone whom they look up to. It's a healthy relationship, not an abnormal one.

The abnormal relationship is quite the contrary. When you think more highly of yourself than you ought to think, you've made yourself your own leader in the Lord. You've set yourself up in a form of pride. Of course, that's justifiable, but then again, anything is justifiable when your heart and head aren't right and you're not lined up with the Scriptures.

SUBORDINATES

Let's go back to the people whom we least like to have correct us—our subordinates. I can't imagine my son when he was 12 years old coming to me and sitting me down and saying, "Dad, I love you, but I don't like the way you're ruling this home. I don't like the way that you're speaking to me. I don't like your tone of voice. I don't know who you think you are! I don't know why you and Mom exalt yourselves as the leadership of this home."

I know this sounds silly. I just can't imagine this ever happening. Yet, in the local church setting we see where the flock—the sheep of God's pasture—does treat the shepherd in such a way. Yet we read in the Scriptures continually that God gave these shepherds and ministry gifts to train, perfect, lead, guide, and guard the people under their authority.

I cannot imagine my daughter (when she was a teenager) confronting me, saying, "I cleaned my room just like you told me to, but I would appreciate it if, when you instruct me to do things like this in the future, you would use a quieter and humbler tone of voice. I did not appreciate the look on your face when you gave me this order."

This is absurd, my friend. The average parent would not put up with this, and I believe that the average teenager would never approach their parents in such a way. Neither should sheep approach leadership in such a way.

It's not that the leadership of the church is untouchable or cannot be spoken to by subordinates. It's just that we have to learn that we cannot be caught up in dissension, cause strife and division, or purposely try to dethrone the governments of God's Kingdom.

You make your pastor your subordinate when the church board rules over him or the congregational vote rules over him. You make your pastor your subordinate even when you feel in your heart that you're greater than he is or when your attitude is, "I know more than he does. I am led of the Spirit as well as, if not better than, he is. I could do a better job than he does. If I were the king . . ." These are the things that can harm you drastically in the Kingdom.

You and I both know, as I've well illustrated so far,

that the minute that your pastor and Christian leaders become your subordinates (either in your mind or in your heart), you are no longer in the position to (and will not) humble yourself to the degree that they will be able to come and reprove you, rebuke you, instruct you, or correct you. Therefore, you have almost negated their ministry in your life. You have made them nothing but a hired voice (a hireling) in their relationship to you. Check yourself out and see if this has begun to happen to you toward some minister of the gospel who is in leadership over your life.

PEERS

The second group or classification of people that you least like to have correct you is your peer group. Many people want to make their pastor a peer, equal to them in authority. Now let's establish the fact that, in the Lord Jesus, we're all totally equal. He loves us all the same. We all have the same opportunities, the same benefits.

He is a God who is no respecter of persons. However, this same God who is not a respecter of persons *does* delegate different levels of authority to go along with the different levels of responsibility that He has placed in people's lives. The pastor has been given the responsibility of guarding the flock. The flock, scripturally, has not been given the responsibility of guarding the pastor.

The pastor (as well as the other fivefold ministry gifts) has been given the responsibility of feeding and equipping and maturing the saints. Nowhere does it say in the Bible that the sheep are to equip, mature, perfect, and train the fivefold ministry gifts. Immediately we have a problem when pastor and people or fivefold ministry gifts and believers become peers and, in their minds, equal in authority.

Let me illustrate a little further here. Many of you, of course, have friends. When your friends come to you seeing something that needs to be adjusted in your life or something wrong with your attitude or your mouth, they'll say something to you *because* they're your friends. Sad to say, the usual response is: "I thought you were my friend. How dare you get in my affairs like this. Who do you think you are? Why do you exalt yourself above me, thinking that now you are holier than me or that you have authority over me?"

We do not expect these things coming from our peers. We expect our peers to be our buddies and our pals. We expect them to understand us and to put up with us, overlooking the negative things in our lives. Once again, we put ourselves in a very dangerous position when we allow our pastor to become our peer.

Now let's establish another thing here. We are not exalting apostles, prophets, evangelists, pastors, and teachers above anything or anyone else. We're using the word "esteem" in the context of showing respect or submitting. This is very clear in the Scriptures. When you read the following passages of scripture, you will get some insight on this particular word:

Scripture references: Jeremiah 3:15, Jeremiah 23:4, 1 Thessalonians 5:12-13, Hebrews 13:17, and Ephesians 4:11-14.

If in the future you do have the opportunity to spend time with people who are fivefold ministry gifts (those truly ordained of God), enjoy that special time that you have. I'm sure that they're enjoying the special time that they have with you because most of them recognize that you are supportive and are ministry of helps to them, but guard your heart and be sure that you do not hurt yourself by losing respect and esteem for them.

Be careful to keep yourself in proper balance and keep yourself always in a student-like, learning situation. This can only enhance and advance you in the Kingdom of God and beautify your relationship with your Lord and King, Jesus Christ.

LEADERSHIP

The third classification of people that we least like to be corrected by is, of course, our leadership. The truth is we don't like to be corrected, but we need it. God knows that we need it. The Bible teaches us that we need it and that God will be sure we get it because it keeps us clean and upright. It keeps us marching in proper order, and it keeps us from becoming polluted and marked (or marred) by the world.

God wants us without spot, wrinkle, blemish, or any such thing. He wants us well trained, knowledgeable, full of wisdom, and not ignorant of spiritual things. He wants us to be walking in and enjoying spiritual things. Leadership should not always be correcting, reproving, and rebuking. However, when we need it, we need it. We should not blame the leadership for it.

There was a man who was speeding on the freeway—excessively so. He was pulled over by a patrolman. When the officer came to the window and asked for the man's driver's license, the man inside the vehicle immediately began to lash out at the officer, calling him names and blaming him for pulling him over. The man in the vehicle said, "Don't you have a murderer to chase? Don't you have more important things to do than to hinder my life? Why are you harassing me? Why did you pick *me* out of all of these drivers?"

You know, this is somewhat of a silly illustration, but I guess at the same time it's very fitting. This is what many sheep do when the pastor comes to deal with them for violating rules of the Kingdom. They feel they are being personally picked on and that the pastor does not love or respect them or that he has just picked them personally out of the crowd to publicly humiliate them.

The man on the freeway was speeding. If he had not been speeding, the officer would not have selected him to be the one he publicly pulled over and began to deal with in correction. It was not the officer's fault. The officer did what was right in the line of his duty. He was upholding the rules and the laws and was also concerned for the safety and well being of the speeder and those who were being sped around.

This is true in the situation of the flock of God. Please don't blame your leadership when they come to deal with your life. Even if you feel it is unfair, be humble and receive it. If you have to, just say to yourself, Let the righteous smite me, and I will consider it as though they were anointing me with oil (Ps. 141:5).

FRIENDS

I want to add here in this chapter on dissension, that *who* your friends are and *whom* you run with, fellowship with, and sup with have *all to do with who and what you are!*

The Bible says in 1 Corinthians 15:33:

"Be not deceived: evil communications corrupt good manners."

I've had people tell me through the years, "Well, Jesus supped with publicans and sinners." Yes, He did, and if you have the results that He did (getting them converted, getting back tax money, and building the Kingdom of God), I would recommend that you do the same thing, for that would be evidence and proof that God has called you to that particular ministry. If you are not getting these results, then you should guard yourself, extremely so. Otherwise, right when you think it's okay for you to be around those particular people, whether they are friends or relatives, you'll find that they're wearing off on you.

They're going to corrupt your good morals. Sooner or later, they're going to influence you. They're going to get into your head, and they're going to change your heart attitude. You're going to turn from sweet to bitter. You're going to turn from confident to suspicious. You're going to turn from submitted to rebellious. You're going to turn from light to dark.

It's been proven, my friend, many, many times over. All of those who have found themselves in this situation also confessed that it would never happen to them, but I'm telling you, whom you sup with and whom you fellowship with and whom you are constantly listening to—this is whom you'll begin to sound like. This is whom you'll begin to act like. Guard yourself.

CHAPTER 4
ABORTING MIRACLES

Why am I making such a big deal out of this? Because it *is* a big deal. It is very, very dangerous, and as I've said in a previous portion of this book, it is like a plague. It runs from the heart of one believer to the heart of another, from the mouth of one believer to the mouth of another, through the head of one sheep, to the heads of the other people attending church. It begins to be a very destructive, very disruptive disease. It literally harms people and makes them weak as Christians. Some even die, it seems, a spiritual death.

Today there is so much being said about the shame of the abortion of unborn babies in the "natural" realm. Some march against it and fight to preserve these babies. I believe we should fight for their lives. But at the same time we are fighting for their lives, some believers are aborting God's seed in their own hearts and lives.

In Matthew 13:53-58 (our text, found in chapter 1 of this book), you will see that because these people "equalized" the authority of the Master Teacher, the Lord Jesus Christ, you could say they aborted the miracles. They did this by viewing Him in their minds and in their hearts as one who received wisdom and did mighty works from somewhere else rather than God. They thought that He was off-base and out of perspective with their way of viewing things. As a result of this, He could not do many miracles there because of their unbelief.

The unbelief was a fruit of their familiarity. They purposely familiarized themselves with pettiness and with simple carnal statements that had no intelligence involved in them whatsoever. They purposed among themselves. Some actually stood up and spoke.

They decided that they did not have to follow these teachings, that they were not necessarily from Heaven. Because of this mind-set and the condition of their hearts, they were no longer receivers of what was being said. Therefore, what was being said had no power in their lives. Because they wouldn't receive what was being said, there was no display of power. There were no mighty miracles for them to witness. There were just a few outbursts of miracles—probably where Jesus, on His own, could break through to those few who were hungering for and believing in Him.

As they reasoned among themselves and certain ones stood up to say contrary things to take away His favor and strip Him of His authority, it began to strip Him of His opportunity to "flex His muscles," to flow in His gift, and to manifest the divine presence of His Father's nature.

CHAPTER 5
THE NAME OF A PROPHET

I'm going to write something here that I know some people will have trouble with because they are not open-minded. I'm sure that others will have trouble with what I have to say because they are rebellious. Others will have trouble because they really live in this sin of excessive familiarity. Others will have trouble with this because they are jealous and envy leadership and just can't stand the fact that God has appointed men (and gifted them) to help the Body of Christ. Along with that, these particular men receive favor, and they receive support from other members of the Body.

> *"He who receives a prophet in the name of a prophet shall receive a prophet's reward; and he who receives a righteous man in the name of a righteous man shall receive a righteous man's reward.*
>
> *And whoever in the name of a disciple gives to one of these little ones even a cup of cold water to drink, truly I say to you he shall not lose his reward."*
>
> Matthew 10:41-42 (NAS)

This is a very famous portion of scripture and is quoted often. It is one that almost every believer has heard at one time or another and has probably even heard a sermon on. I'm not going to attempt to preach a new sermon on it here, especially not in the setting of this book, but I would like to refer to it and perhaps show you a couple of pieces of wisdom that may aid you personally.

This says that if you receive a prophet in the name of a prophet, you will receive a prophet's reward. Let's examine it. If you receive a prophet in the name of a prophet, then you will receive a prophet's reward. Many people misquote this, and their mind-set is off. That's why they are not receiving the prophet's reward. Most of us go to listen to the prophet and get his hands laid upon us because we want that reward. We need it; it's from Heaven. It's a gift to us, and we want it in our lives.

Why don't we have it? Because many of us have misquoted and misread the scriptures. We misquote it like this: "He who receives a prophet in the name of a prophet's *God* will receive the prophet's reward." Here's another misquote: "He who receives a prophet in the name of Jesus receives a prophet's reward."

The idea of this scripture is *receiving*. If you do not receive a man, though he's gifted of God and sent of God to aid you, you'll not receive from him all that he has for you. If you're suspicious or critical of him or if you don't trust him, don't respect him, won't submit to him, don't honor him, question what he speaks, question his lifestyle, etc., how will you ever receive what he says as though it's from the throne room?

The truth is that you will not. You will examine everything and most likely become very critical of his ministry rather than honor him. If you receive a prophet in the name of a prophet, you'll receive the gift of that prophet: for example, if you receive Mark Barclay in the name of Mark Barclay, you'll receive the gift that God put in me to deliver to you.

Now don't get upset yet, let me finish this. On the contrary, if you do not receive me, if you are suspicious of me, critical of me, judgmental toward me, and are leary of me and have mistrust toward me, then everything I say to you, you'll receive only partially. You'll receive it screened. You'll want to filter the things that I present to you and, in essence, you'll be robbed of what I've really come to bring you out of the gift that God has placed in me according to Ephesians 4.

Let me illustrate this further. In the late 1970s and early 1980s, I attended some camp meetings where a powerful preacher and teacher of our time, Kenneth E. Hagin, was ministering. I would notice that many, many people came from all over the nation and other parts of the world to be in these camp meetings. They came to hear Kenneth E. Hagin. They came to hear from the prophet. They came to hear in the name of that prophet.

You knew they came to hear from Kenneth E. Hagin because on the nights that he was speaking, they'd fill the auditorium up. They would come early. They would park two or three miles away. They would stand in line for hours. They would put their coats and Bibles on chairs, whatever they had to do to get a seat early, close to the prophet.

In many of their minds this was not exaltation of a man, not at all. This was only esteeming an officer of God's Kingdom. They knew that a gift was placed in him by the Head of the Church, and they wanted to put a draw upon that gift. They wanted to be there early. Most of them came, as I mentioned before, to receive from Kenneth E. Hagin. You knew this the following morning at 10 a.m. when someone else was scheduled to teach and preach. Many of the mass crowd slept in, ate breakfast, and went shopping. There were very few people standing in line for a chair.

Why? Not because that speaker was not as good a teacher, not because God loved Kenneth E. Hagin more than these other teachers, nor for any of the other reasons we might be able to give. No, it was because those people journeyed all of those miles to receive from the prophet, Kenneth E. Hagin, in the name of his ministry, Kenneth E. Hagin Ministries. It was *his* hands they wanted laid upon them. They came to hear *his* voice, to receive from the gift that God put in *him*.

I know some people have trouble with this. Some people think that this is stretching it too far, but I'm telling you, friend (and I'm not afraid to take the risk to tell you), that the reason that many of you have not received fully from your pastors and from the other ministry gifts, is that you do not receive them in their own names. Sure, you trust the name of Jesus. Sure, you trust the Word of the Lord, and most of you trust yourselves, but when it comes down to trusting another man and honoring his name, we begin to have immediate problems. Many of us begin to withdraw from even the idea.

Some people may wonder since their pastor isn't a prophet, how this affects them. Well, the verse goes on to say, "He that receives a righteous man in the name of a righteous man receives a righteous man's reward." So the same thing is true. If you are suspicious and critical and judgmental and leary about your pastor and his lifestyle and who he is, if you become too familiar with him, or if you tear down what esteem you may have had for him, you are not going to receive from him anywhere near what you would receive from him if you did not have these negative elements in your life.

Two people can sit and listen to the same sermon preached by the same man. One will be totally resurrected by the sermon, while the other person dies spiritually. Why? Because one has made himself a peer; one has made himself a critic, a judge, an investigator, suspicious, collecting information. One simply came to receive the man in his name, respecting him as a person, then tapping into the supernatural gift of God that was placed within him that he might grow thereby.

Check yourself. Are you receiving the prophet in the name of a prophet? Are you receiving the righteous man in the name of a righteous man, or have you been deceived into thinking that this is some sort of weird error that you should beware of? Let's keep in mind here that we're talking about godly leadership in the area of teaching, not about cultish leaders penetrating your homes and private lives, demanding and commanding things that they really do not have dominion over.

We're talking here about a teaching setting, a leadership setting, where you come to learn and to listen and to be fed. Then we, the leadership, simply do what Paul did in the Book of Acts—commend you to God's Word, and that Word is able to keep you and bring you into the inheritance of Christ and to guide you along the way.

CHAPTER 6
THE THREE ZONES OF LIFE

CONFIDENCE ZONE SUSPICION ZONE FAMILIARITY ZONE

There are three zones of life. Either people have never learned this or they neglect to live by it though they may have knowledge of it. The three zones of life are as I've illustrated at the top of this page: 1) the Suspicion Zone, which is where you always start, 2) the Confidence Zone, where God expects you to live, and 3) the Familiarity Zone, where you begin to get into trouble, form bad attitudes, and become displeasing in the sight of the Father.

The Suspicion Zone is that area where you come in and you begin to ask questions. It's the area where you accumulate information. It's that area where you begin to build a relationship. It's that area where you are pioneering or you are considered a rookie. The Suspicion Zone is that area where you're not familiar enough to understand people or have a relationship with them. This is not unfair. All of us must spend a certain amount of time in the Suspicion Zone collecting information. Once we have that information, we should enter into the Confidence Zone.

The Confidence Zone is where God honors and

blesses us. This is where the flourishing is because we are not judgmental or critical. We're not suspicious. We're not irreverent, rather we're submitted, we're bold, and we're well able (because of relationship and trust) to do all that God has called us to do. We are able to walk in right relationship with other people in what God has called them to do, even in our lives. You can sink, however, into excessive familiarity and lose your reverence, lose your esteem, and lose your respect for God, His house, His Word, His men, the rest of His people, and even yourselves.

Each of us, in every phase of life, must come through the Suspicion Zone at first to collect information in order to build relationships. We then enter into the Confidence Zone, where we function and perform properly in the sight of the Lord. Once there, we must guard ourselves that we don't divert back to the Suspicion Zone or that we don't get into excessive familiarity and get ourselves in trouble. Let's look at this a little closer.

THE SUSPICION ZONE

This is the zone, or area of life, where you collect information. This is where you begin to build relationship. This is where you talk out initial differences. This is where you make determinations of whether or not you're going to walk in relationship with certain things, principles, companies, or people. This is where you determine if you will walk in relationship as sheep to shepherd. I'll give some actual illustrations of this later on in this book.

You must take the time to go through this Zone of Suspicion or you'll find that you will have to come back to it later. Many people, in the dating relationship between a man and a woman or in the working relationship between employer and employee, make covenants together without actually examining one another and all of the details that are involved. Later on, after they've tried to work out this covenant and walk together, they realize that they have many questions and many things that were not discussed, settled, and agreed upon during the time that they should have been.

The time period in which these things should have been discussed is what I call the Suspicion Zone. You're a little suspicious of each other, both partners in the covenant, so you question and gather information. It is expected that as you gather this information, you work out differences, you agree on detail, and you begin to build relationship. This is proper and upright. This is not wrong. The wrong and the harm come when you try to walk in the Confidence Zone prematurely and then have to return back into the Zone of Suspicion to redo the foundation of your relationship.

THE CONFIDENCE ZONE

The Confidence Zone is that area of life, mind-set, and attitude of heart where you and I are to live. It's the zone where God blesses, honors, and rewards us. It's the zone of life where the fruit of the Spirit comes forth, where the gifts of the Spirit are allowed to flow without abnormality, and where we are allowed to walk in full joy and peace because this is where we have confidence.

The Bible says, "Cast not away, therefore, your confidence, for it brings us a great reward." God expects us to walk in pure faith. This is the area where we walk, believing and trusting in God and His leadership, His Word, His appointed men who are leaders in the house of the Lord, and each other. This is the area of relationship that we have with other people, where we're not constantly suspicious or critical of them, but we trust them even when we may hear or see things that would cause us to have alarm if we were walking in a lesser relationship.

God wants us to walk in the zone of life called "Confidence." It is not that difficult to live there, however there *is* some warfare involved. Satan will constantly try to push you out. Imagine being "King of the Mountain." You're on the mountaintop, and satan wants your position. He wants to push you backward into the Zone of Suspicion or forward into the Zone of Familiarity. If he can push you backward, he has begun to destroy relationships, causing you to once again question and doubt—losing out because you don't walk in faith, believing the things of the Kingdom.

He will also try to push you forward into the excessive Familiarity Zone where you begin to become overly critical. You begin to become too familiar, and you slowly lose respect and esteem because you have made your leadership your peer or you have made God your prayer buddy or you have made His Word just another book that you read.

Guard yourself in order to stay in this Confidence Zone. Do what is biblically right. Guard whom you fellowship with, guard that you keep your covenants and your word with other people. Guard your heart, hiding His Word there that you don't sin against Him. Guard your heart, for out of it flow the issues of life. Guard your mouth. Put a guard upon your lips. The Bible says that you can have what you say. You can enjoy the fruit of your lips. You're justified or condemned by the words of your lips, and life and death are in the power of the tongue. If you and I would just be good and faithful stewards of the mysteries of God, we would constantly war and fight, pushing the devil forward and backward instead of him pushing us, and we would stay in this Confidence Zone where God truly blesses.

THE FAMILIARITY ZONE

The Zone of excessive Familiarity is the one that most of us find ourselves plunging into. I don't think we mean to, but quite often we find ourselves there. We have come through the Suspicion Zone, asking the questions and building the relationships properly. We know what it's like now to walk in the Confidence Zone, but satan, not being able to push us backward into that kind of doubt and unbelief, will have the tendency to try to push us forward into this excessive familiarity.

This is where we begin to take advantage and take for granted the wonderful, beautiful blessings in our lives. This sort of excessive familiarity is where children begin to doubt parents in their teenage years. This is where husbands begin to become critical and judgmental of their wives and vice versa (wives to husbands). This is where sheep slowly begin to lose esteem and respect for their leaders after they've been in a particular church for a while. This is where the leaders begin to do the same thing toward their leadership and toward their people. This is where we, as believers, even begin to treat God, His Word, and His house less respectfully than we should.

Making ourselves familiar is proper. Familiarizing ourselves in the form of knowledge and building relationships is proper and upright, and God expects it. That will put you up in the Confidence Zone, as I illustrated earlier. However, there is a place where you become too familiar—

to the excess. It's where we begin to grumble and complain and lose our satisfaction with the very things that we once prayed for. I'm going to show you this on the following pages by giving you some illustrations. Remember, there are three zones of life.

CHAPTER 7
LIFE'S EXAMPLES

NEW CAR EXAMPLE

Let me give you another example—a new car. Many of us have the privilege from time to time to buy a new automobile or at least a fresh, used automobile. When you first buy that automobile, you check it out really well. When you go to that dealer, you're in the Suspicion Zone. You don't know who he is; you don't trust him. You haven't built a relationship with him, perhaps.

You want to know about this car. Who owned it before, if anyone? What kind of warranty does it have? What kind of tires are these? Can you open the hood? What kind of engine is under here? Is this leather or vinyl on these seats? What kind of fuel mileage does it get?

These are all questions that you ask, trying to get your suspicions soothed and taken care of so that you can feel confident about owning and driving this vehicle. After you purchase it, you take very good care of it. You like it. You cherish it. Some of you even drive in front of store windows looking at its reflection, saying to yourself how well you look in it and how glad you are you made the purchase.

You're so proud of this new vehicle, but you know, if you're not careful, you'll fall into that excessive Familiarity Zone. You'll begin to grumble and complain about the very thing that you believed God for, the very thing that you cherished, the gift that came to you. You'll even make negative comments about its manufacturer. You'll wish you didn't have it.

Your eyes will be drawn to another vehicle. You'll already be meditating about a replacement but have feelings that you're bound by the one that you have. When you first had it, it was spic and span. You would hardly let anyone touch it. You kept all of the raindrops polished off it and all the tires clean.

Now you just drive it, and many times it's dirty. You even leave drive-in food and drinks on the interior. Somehow I can't help but think that God admires us when we live and walk in confidence and take care of things. I believe that God has trouble with us and we're not so pleasing to Him when He sees us abusing and grumbling about the very things that we once asked for and that became our blessing and that we were thrilled about.

EMPLOYMENT EXAMPLE

As a pastor and a Christian leader, I've watched many people come into the church without employment, hurting financially, fighting poverty and lack. We pray with them and believe with them to get jobs. I've seen many of these people fill out their applications and fast and pray and ask God for employment that they might take care of their families. I've watched God move and supply these jobs.

I've watched other men leave jobs and start their own

businesses, advancing in life, becoming their own employers, their own bosses, starting their own companies. I've watched how these people pray, get through all the suspicion and all the questions they have, and overcome all the fear to get up into the Confidence Zone.

These people go into these new jobs, and the first day on the job, they ask a lot of questions: "When do we punch in? When do we punch out? Where are the bathrooms? Where do we eat lunch? Are we allowed to take any coffee breaks during the day? Who is the manager? Who is my supervisor? What if I get hurt? What if I need a day off?" Question after question is asked, that they might understand those details, work out the differences, and come to an agreement so that they can have confidence that this job is right. They can then perform in that confidence and be the best employee, perhaps, in the company.

When they examined this job (in suspicion), wanting it to be theirs, the mileage didn't matter. They didn't care that they had to drive an hour to get there. They knew the car would hold up. They knew God had given them this job. They were believing for it. They had their faith on it. They didn't care about the conditions that they'd be working in, because they knew that God was giving them this job. They felt good about it. They were confident, so they went for it.

God did answer their prayers, and they did start this business or get this job. These same people who fasted and prayed and asked God (and all these little details did not matter to them) become slowly dissatisfied. They become excessively familiar, and they begin to grumble about the boss and complain about the working conditions. Each night before they go to bed, they make negative comments to their spouse about how far it is to drive. They wish they had a better job, cleaner working conditions, a boss who liked them, more pay, etc.

MARRIAGE EXAMPLE

Each of you who is married had to—before you were married—build a relationship and become confident in that relationship. You had to become confident that the person you were courting or were becoming engaged to was, indeed, the person whom you wanted to live with for the rest of your life. Most Christians realize that the marriage covenant should be for the entirety of their lives and that God does not favor and is not the cause of divorce or nullification of such covenants.

When that man first came and put the move on you, winked at you, and said things to you, all of you women were on guard. You were suspicious. Who is this guy? When you dated him, went out with him, or perhaps the first time he kissed you, you liked it, but you said to yourself, “Who is this guy? How dare he make this advance, this penetration, into my private life?” You were suspicious. You asked a lot of questions. He asked a lot of questions about you. You had to work out differences. You had to come to agreement on details. Some of you women said to that young man, “I want to meet your father.” He asked why, and you said, “I want to see what you’re going to look like when you’re 45 or 50 years old.” (Ha ha.)

You see, all of us did things similar to this in building our relationships until one day we came to an area of confidence where we began to say—even publicly, “This is the man for me.” “This is the woman for me.” “We are engaged.”

God wants us to stay in that Confidence Zone. He wants us cherishing, trusting, flourishing, and enjoying our relationship one with the other. God enjoys it. He answers our prayers, the Bible says, so that our joy may be full. Here we are married. God's answered our prayers. We've worked out the details of courtship. We've worked out the details of commitment. We've worked out our differences that we might find a place to come together, not only in the walk of life but also in intimacy.

Now we find ourselves complaining. We begin to distrust one another. We nitpick and become very petty. She talks about the way he leaves clothes lying around. He talks about the way she burns the toast and doesn't fry the eggs right. These things, of course, are always very petty and very selfish but so damaging. They literally destroy marriages if they are meditated on long enough.

Do you know why? Not because they are big issues but because this is a big sin. It's a heart problem. No matter what the other person says to fix it, the heart problem of excessive familiarity is so damaging that it blurs the vision and blinds the mind. You begin to grumble and complain. You begin to show irreverence. You lose your respect and esteem for the person whom you once walked with in great pleasure.

Because of this sin of familiarity, many people end up in divorce and abandonment. This is a shame, because if they had stayed up in the Confidence Zone, all these things could have been worked out.

CHURCH EXAMPLE

Let's take this same principle and apply it to the

church setting. We've talked about possessions. We've talked about employer and employee relationships. We've talked about personal and marital/intimate relationships. Now, let's examine how this shows up in church life.

Many of us were so hungry for what God had for us, we began to search out where He was moving. Most of us had to stretch out and reach out to find it. We prayed. We asked God. We were hungry! We drove miles. We flew miles to get to a place where we could be fed and worship and praise and get in the flow of the Spirit of God.

Do you know that when we first come to a church and first sit under a pastor, we are in the Suspicion Zone? This is proper, not abnormal. There's nothing wrong with it. We must ask a lot of questions. That's fair and honest. People should give us answers. We should ask, "Where is the restroom? Where is the nursery? What do you believe here? What are the cardinal doctrines of this church? Who is the pastor? Where was he educated? Who are his friends? What does he stand for? What are the issues of this church? What is its vision? What is its future? What are we for? What are we against?"

This is all part of being suspicious. It's all part of collecting information so that we can build a proper relationship. But as we attend that church, going through the membership classes, doctrine classes, or orientation classes, we gather information that gives us confidence. We begin to build a more intimate relationship. We begin to trust the leadership. We begin to trust the people of the church. We begin to adopt the vision. Sooner or later we begin to call it our church, and we begin to call the man who is pastoring there our shepherd.

This is how we build relationship. We should have had all of our questions answered. We should feel confident. We should jump up into the Confidence Zone and begin to work with those other laborers as they build, witness, evangelize, sow good seed, do the work, and fulfill the vision of that church because we are now one of them.

We are now confident that this is where God wants us. We asked Him for it. He led us here. The details and the differences have been worked out to the degree that we can live in relationship—giving and taking, sowing and reaping, laughing and crying, bearing our own burdens and bearing one another's burdens also—this is church life!

God begins to flourish us here. Our hearts are right, our minds are clean, our mouths are upright. Things begin to work for us. God feeds us and we enjoy it. It's a wonderful and marvelous thing. This is where God intends for us to live and stay. However, it isn't too long for some, a little longer for others, until this familiarity—this wicked sin—begins to work and show up in people's lives.

When we first started attending this church, we probably said, "It's not too far to drive. It won't be too bad. The car will last. God will give us extra grace. Just like the children in the wilderness whose shoes did not wear out, so we'll believe that our tires will not wear out." We made big commitments. We said big things to God and to each other. We were sure! We were confident this was where God wanted us.

Now after a season, this sin begins to work in our heads and in our hearts. Our mouths begin to proclaim it. We begin to grumble about how far it is to drive. The services go too long or it's too hot or it's too cold. The chairs are not comfortable enough. The music is too loud or too quiet. We collect excuses a mile long, but the problem is not the place. The problem is not the distance, it's not the music, it's not the preacher, it's not the chairs, and it's not the climate.

None of these things ever hindered us before, when we were up in the Confidence Zone. We simply overcame and overlooked them and kept on growing and going in God. Now that we have the sin operating in our hearts, we begin to produce unbelief. We begin to nullify.

If we're not careful, we'll soon divorce the church, the pastor, and the work. We'll run somewhere else out of despair. We'll begin to grumble and complain, criticize, and become judgmental about the ministry gift that's there and about the way things are said and done.

God listens and says, "I thought they asked Me to come here. I thought they enjoyed it here." You see, God monitors us and begins to say, "Why are they disrespectful? Why are they rebellious? Why are they stiffnecked? Why are they so selfish and critical? Why are they judging the way that they are?"

It is a sin to have a heart condition like this, a mind that wanders like this, and lips that pronounce such things as we do when we're dissatisfied. Disrespect, irreverence, and a critical spirit begin to grip us. This sin begins to drag us away, like sheep to the slaughter. This is not God's will for us. It is never God's will for us to fall into the sin of familiarity and turn into people whom He has to deal with in ways that He shouldn't have to deal with sons and daughters.

Be a grateful person. Be thankful. Guard your heart. I

challenge you, again, to watch your lips. Cherish the things God has given you—the people in your life, your family, your church leadership.

Guard your attitude toward the house of God, the Word of God, offerings, worship, praise, and prayer. Come out of that Suspicion Zone. Walk in confidence. Be bold and watch God flourish you and bless you in His garden.

CHAPTER 8
BIBLE EXAMPLES

Let's march on in this book and look at some Bible examples. The examples I've given you here are very simple, down-to-earth, and practical. Many people have wondered if this sin can be found in the Bible other than in this passage of scripture in Matthew about Jesus in the synagogue in Nazareth.

The answer is, yes it can. With a very short explanation I am going to show you some different examples in the Bible. That, of course, will inspire you to search for yourself. You will find many, many more times where excessive familiarity actually is operating as a sin in even some of the "best" Bible characters.

AARON—TOO FAMILIAR

Aaron was chosen and approved by God as the mouthpiece for Moses. They worked together in tough times and in good times. Aaron was like Moses' right-hand man. Moses would show him things and speak things to him. Aaron would be the spokesman and stand up on behalf of Moses and declare them.

Aaron was a priest. He was a well-respected man. He

had a wonderful position, you might say, as the number two man in the realm of sacraments and authority in the ministry of Moses. We read, however, that even Aaron in his strength and confidence got into trouble and fell into this sin of familiarity.

Moses went to the mount to be with God, to see who He was, in the cloud 40 days and 40 nights. While Moses was gone, Aaron began to listen to the people. People got to his heart. They got to his head first, I'm sure. They began to persuade him to do other than what his knowledge and experience told him to do. The integrity of his heart began to fall. He found himself alone with those who had a better idea, those who did not want to follow the leadership in Moses' absence, those who wanted to worship in a manner other than what was prescribed by the leadership.

You know the story. They worshiped, they praised, they sang. They melted down all of their gems and jewels and precious metals. They made themselves an idol, a brazen calf, and they began to worship it.

As you know, when Moses came down from the mountain, he was angry! When he confronted Aaron, I can just hear Aaron trying to justify how he lost respect for his position. He had lost respect for Moses' word (out-of-sight/out-of-mind type of thinking). He tried to explain how the people had persuaded him on the spot to be less than what he really was.

Aaron got in trouble with the people that day and got the people in trouble. He was supposed to be mature enough and have enough integrity to hold things in order in the absence of the number one man who was in the presence of the Lord.

Aaron, instead of maintaining order, allowed the people to rule over him. They overcame him. They intimidated him. They persuaded him. The fact that he was a little bit too familiar with Moses' voice, a little bit too close to this man whom he worked with, a little bit too familiar with his office and his responsibilities, resulted in him being persuaded. This is how Aaron fell into this horrible position.

MIRIAM—TOO FAMILIAR

Miriam, a woman of the Lord, walked closely with Moses. She was related to him but was also in leadership. She was constantly found as support at the front of the scene walking and talking with the leadership in God's camp. We see the account in the Old Testament, however, how one day she began to force her differences and disagreements with Moses, God's number one leader, there in the camp. Notice he wasn't the only leader, but he was the senior leader on the staff.

Miriam persuaded some others and began to talk. She and Aaron talked. She could not keep confidence. She could not keep respect for who she was and the privileges that she had. She lost track of the position and the blessings that were bestowed upon her, and she began to grumble and complain about the very things that she did not have. She lost respect for Moses. She lost esteem for him. She began to grumble and say, "Does God only speak through Moses?"

We always seem to somehow forget that the number one person listening to us is God. God heard Miriam and Aaron. God came down that day and called all three of them (Miriam, Aaron, and Moses) out. God dealt with the issue. He called Miriam and Aaron out even farther. He allowed leprosy to be put upon Miriam, and Aaron had to bear the reproach of it. It stopped the whole move of God for days as they waited for Miriam to be cleansed of this leprosy and be restored back into the camp.

God made Himself very clear here. He will not put up with the sin of familiarity robbing us. He will not put up with murmuring and grumbling and corrupt communication. He will not put up with the challenging of leadership by those with critical spirits and judgmental attitudes. God is still this way today. I'll show you in the next few pages even some New Testament illustrations of how God deals with people.

Miriam lost out. Yes, she was restored, but she had to bear the pain and the reproach for coming out of the Zone of Confidence. She had come out of that zone of gratitude and respect and fallen into excessive familiarity. She had allowed herself to become too familiar with God, His blessings, His privileges, and His leadership.

GEHAZI—TOO FAMILIAR

Gehazi is another Old Testament illustration of a man who really had a beautiful position. He was like the number two person in "Elisha Ministries," second only to one of the greatest prophets in the land. Gehazi was his servant, or assistant. Elisha trusted him. He trained him. They worked together. They were partners and colaborers in the Kingdom of God.

Gehazi was sent to cleanse Naaman, the great army general, of leprosy. Gehazi was sent to raise a son who had died in the field. Elisha, the prophet, really trusted this man and delegated some very strong responsibilities to him and expected him to fulfill them.

Gehazi began to be ministered to by this sin of familiarity. In other words, it began to show up in his heart. His vision changed just a little bit (his perspective on things is what I mean). One day it really showed up. When that army general was cleansed of leprosy, he came back to give a reward to the prophet. The prophet turned him down and sent him away.

You see, the prophet knew that if he received the money, the general would have gone everywhere, telling people that this "Elisha Ministries" had the power to cleanse lepers. He would have had every leper from all over sitting on his doorstep or calling out to him for help. Though that in itself wouldn't have been bad, what would have hurt is that it would have taken Elisha off course and would have taken him into a form or realm of ministry that was not God's intention for him to have. He sent that general away not accepting the gift.

Gehazi, in excessive familiarity, looked at the old prophet kind of funny. He judged him and criticized him in his heart a little bit for his decision. He wondered why he hadn't taken the gift. If he didn't want it, why hadn't he received it and given it to his faithful servant, Gehazi?

In private, Gehazi ran after that army general. He said, "The prophet changed his mind. He's had some sojourners since you left, and he needs some garments and some blessing." Gehazi took some belongings and some treasure from the general. He ran home and hid it in his tent under his bed and went to work the next day thinking that the prophet would never know.

You know, that's the problem. Many people think, The leadership will never know; God's not watching. The very fact that Gehazi had these garments meant he would never have been able to wear them without the prophet noticing that they were new and that they came from a different land, the land of Naaman. When and what would he have spent this treasure on without the prophet knowing that he had more treasure than what he had received through the ministry that he worked for?

Again, once he begins to commit this sin of familiarity, we find a great lack of intelligence in a man who was known for his character.

Elisha confronted Gehazi the next time they were together. He said, "What have you been up to, Gehazi? Don't you know that my heart was with you, my spirit was with you, when you stood at the general's chariot and received those blessings from him?"

Gehazi was blown away that Elisha knew everything. That's the way some people are today. They're blown away that the leadership really knows things about them. God watches us. He listens, and He warns those who have been placed as leaders over our lives. He does this to help us and correct us and to keep us straight.

Gehazi ended up with the leprosy that had been upon Naaman. He died with leprosy, and it was passed down to his offspring. Here was a man who had a wonderful opportunity to perhaps be in the ministry and to someday take over one of the greatest ministries of his time. This man died a leper because of his lack of esteem and respect, which grew in him and showed up in him through the sin of familiarity.

JUDAS—TOO FAMILIAR

Jesus allowed Judas to stay with the disciples until the Last Supper. He didn't run him off from the "first supper," but He let him stay until the very last one, feeding from His ministry, learning, and giving him the opportunity to be part of the Kingdom. However, Judas' heart was overwhelmed with jealousy, envy, familiarity, and peer pressure. He began in his heart first to deny Jesus. He ran to the religious rulers and began to play both sides.

We have people like this in our churches today. Eventually, he sold out Christ for money! It wasn't really the money that he wanted, as much as it was the defaming and stripping Jesus of all the favor and respect that He had in the eyes of His followers.

I believe with all of my heart that this was what bothered Judas—Jesus getting more attention than he did. Jesus had more followers and more fame. Judas felt that Jesus was not giving him enough personal time and personal attention, and that ate away at Mr. Iscariot until it began to show up on his lips. Then it showed up in his actions until finally he was confronted by God. We all know the end of that story.

ANANIAS AND SAPPHIRA—TOO FAMILIAR

Ananias and Sapphira were church people, New Testament Church people, after the outpouring of the Holy Ghost, after the resurrection and the ascension of the Lord Jesus Christ. They were people of good reputation. They were respected by many as people who worked in God's Kingdom and in His temple.

Ananias and Sapphira just got too familiar with

offerings and pledging and building funds and giving to the poor and distribution. They just got so familiar with their jobs and their positions that they began to make some mistakes.

Barnabas, another highly-respected man, began to make pledges, as others did also, and he pledged some property. He sold it and brought the money in and gave it to the church. It was a momentum that the church had going, that all things would be common and equal. I believe that Ananias and Sapphira got caught up in this public offering, and they made commitments that were not birthed out of their own hearts. Therefore, when the time came to keep them, they did not do what was right.

They did sell their land. They did come in and give a portion to the church. But this man, Peter, who knew about the sin of familiarity and had been confronted by Christ and the Holy Spirit about it, discerned it, I believe, upon Ananias and Sapphira. He challenged them immediately about their pledge. He wondered why it did not meet the amount that was due. This is unusual in itself, that a man of God would even confront a New Testament believer about giving and tithing. A confrontation like this today would make the headlines!

You know the rest of the story, friend. Ananias and Sapphira both died that day. They fell over because they lied to the Holy Ghost. Really what they did was make commitments to the church and to church leadership but did not keep them. They did not fulfill what they had promised. This was bad news, and it's still bad news for you and me today.

CHAPTER 9
LOCAL CHURCH EXAMPLES

ASSISTANT PASTOR—TOO FAMILIAR

Some people ask, Does this really happen today in churches, or did this just show up in Bible times? The answer is, yes it is still happening today in churches and can be seen. As you've meditated prayerfully in this book, you've seen that this shows up, even in your life, from time to time in different areas. If you don't check it, judge it, guard it, and discard it immediately, it will grow there like any other sin. It will cause you to believe things, feel things, see things, interpret things, and practice things that you normally would not—with a clear mind and under the guidance of the Holy Spirit.

A pastor I know explained the story of a man who came onto his staff to work in an assistant-type role (probably as the assistant pastor). When he first came, he voiced how much he respected the pastor and admired his ministry. He would talk about how he had been fed by this pastor's books and tapes and by his teaching ministry. He voiced that he didn't want any money, he wasn't seeking a position, and he wasn't an authority seeker. He had just come to serve. He wanted to do anything he could. He really did prove himself, outwardly, to the body there, gained favor, and became the assistant pastor.

He hadn't been the assistant very long when he let this sin of familiarity begin to operate in his life. Instead of being grateful and thankful, humble and teachable, serving and growing, and being part of God's blessings and God's things, he began to accumulate negative facts. He began to disagree in his heart. He began to want more attention and demand more respect from the people. He began to lose respect for the senior pastor. His open disagreement with certain things, certain teachings, and certain governmental decisions would even come out of his mouth from time to time.

Slowly, but surely, this death grip, this sin of familiarity, grabbed him by the jugular vein and began to choke him out. His attitude turned sour. He got very disrespectful. His mind began to wander and dream, and he'd perceive things totally off-base. His mouth began to sin tremendously in strife and talebearing and gossip. It began to hurt the church. The pastor finally had to relieve him. It ended that he left that ministry and that local church. He was like a fish out of water, flopping around, trying to believe God for recovery.

It's a horrible sin, this sin of familiarity. It does strange things to your head and your heart. It causes you to say and do things that are really not you and that are not in line with the way that you have normally worked with God and His people.

INTERCESSOR—TOO FAMILIAR

There was an intercessor who had a heart to pray. She

voiced that she had nothing in mind but to pray for the church and to pray for the pastor, so she did. She caused such a momentum that others joined her. It looked like a revival of prayer was breaking out.

The pastor began to sense, however, that the prayers were not being voiced in the right direction. The name of the devil and demons were being used too often. Bits and pieces of revelations and inspirations were being picked up and enhanced. Communication was based on that, and they began to build whole issues. Soon this developed to where the intercessor started coming to the pastor in his office and declaring what they had seen in prayer.

The pastor listened the first couple of times out of courtesy, not realizing that by listening he was providing this intercessor the platform of almost being like a prophetess or a voice from God.

A problem began to develop with this intercessor. She began to look down on the pastor. First in her mind, he was her peer, then he was her subordinate. She began to view herself as the person between the shepherd and the True Shepherd. She began to bring direction, then correction, and when the pastor would not do what she said, she would allow that to bleed down to the other intercessors. Then it bled into the rest of the church until it really began to raise havoc in that local church setting. When the pastor finally confronted her on this issue, she blew up and said that he was not a man of God. She left that church and today is out wandering around, wondering what she really is supposed to be, where she is supposed to be, who she is, and what she should be doing.

If you were to talk to her (of course, this is true with

all people who are in trouble), she would say that everything is fine and she's never had it better. But it is evident by her performance and her lifestyle that this excessive familiarity wreaked more havoc and did more damage than what she even realized was taking place.

SONG LEADER—TOO FAMILIAR

You know, song leaders are in a very different position. They are up in front of the people. They seem to have control of the congregation. They have favor, and people enjoy their ministry because the truth is, most people would rather sing and clap and dance than listen to Bible teaching.

Song leaders have to always guard themselves. Many times the leadership will want to make adjustments, sing longer or shorter, omit a song or add a song, or ask for certain things to take place in the service. Many of the leaders are not musically-oriented or inclined and, of course, the song leader is, so if the song leader or musicians do not check themselves constantly, this sin of familiarity can creep in.

If you are in the music ministry, singing ministry, leading of worship, or leading of spiritual songs, or if you are being used in God's house on your musical instrument, I would like to challenge you as you are reading this paragraph to guard your heart. Don't let this familiarity seep in to where you begin to be a know-it-all or you begin to lean only on your talent or you begin to deny the authority placed over your life. You'll then lose your gratitude and your thankfulness. Don't let yourself operate in this excessive familiarity. It will rob you of your stand for the Lord.

CHAPTER 10
FIGHTING THE SIN

I'd like to give you some helpful Bible hints here on how to fight the sin of familiarity in its earliest stages. If it's already overwhelmed you, you can do nothing but openly repent, go back and patch up whatever damage you've done in local churches with leadership, family members, or friends, and make sure that things are right between you and God and you and those you've harmed.

Prayerfully, this book comes to you before you've done much damage and you'll be able to correct yourself by following some very simple Bible principles.

The first one, of course, is to judge yourself. Commune with your own heart, examining and looking back over the way you've been living, what you've been feeling, and what you've been meditating in. The whole Bible is full of scriptures to support those particular things. Here are some specifics.

BE STEADFAST IN THE FAITH
(James 4:6-7)

That's how we resist the devil, by doing the things related to Christianity—reading our Bibles, going to church, fasting, praying, worshiping, praising, giving, tithing, submitting, and obeying. The devil has very little defense against us when we do that which is right. This also is a guard for your heart, to be more and more involved in the things of God, to walk with God, and be in the Word of God. These are all strong defenses against this sin of familiarity. If you hide His Word in your heart, as the psalmist said, you'll not sin against Him.

DRAW NIGH UNTO GOD (James 4:8)

Draw nigh unto God, and He will draw nigh unto you. This is a wonderful key to staying out of familiarity. The closer you draw unto God, the closer He draws unto you. The more He shows up, the more liberty you have—where the Spirit of the Lord is, there is liberty. Drawing nigh unto God is, however, more than just getting God to show up. It's your heart, mind, and strength—all of it, in fact—pushing into the beauty of holiness, pushing into the throne room. When you're using all of your thoughts and energies and attention to be close with God, you usually don't have much time to meditate in or to be involved in much else.

HUMBLE YOURSELVES (James 4:10)

This is something that you and I have to do. No one can do it for us. It's a heart attitude. It's sitting at someone else's feet. It's realizing that we're not the supremacy of life. It's realizing we're not to think any more highly of ourselves than we ought to think. Humbling ourselves is a way of chuckling at the things we've done in this life that embarrass us and saying, I'll march on anyway! It's a way of admitting that others may know more, or even are to be esteemed and honored more, than ourselves. It's a way to keep learning and to keep this gross sin of familiarity out of our hearts.

WATCH THE COMPANY THAT YOU KEEP (1 Corinthians 15:33)

I've mentioned this before—bad company will corrupt even your good morals. It's of utmost importance that you realize who it is that your friends are and that you do not sup with people who are drawing you away (bitter, rebellious, backslidden, gossiping, talebearing, resentful, critical, judgmental people). Slowly their vocabularies and their attitudes will wear off on you. Even in the strongest of Christians, when these negative seeds are allowed to be sown in us, they'll begin to grow, and we will find ourselves in a battle that we won't want to deal with.

GUARD YOUR HEART (Proverbs 4:23)

Guard your heart, for out of it flow the issues of life. Guard it. Put a guard upon it. Watch what you look at. Watch what you listen to. Let your heart and the emotions of your soul remain stabilized. Set your affections on things that are above. You know, the Bible says that to the pure, all things are pure, but to the defiled, everything in their sight, everything to them, has a defiled look and a defiled taste.

DEAL WITH YOUR HEAD—THOUGHTS (2 Corinthians 10:4-6)

Pull down strongholds. Cast down imaginations. A lot

of things that we think about other people are simply things that we imagine. People really didn't mean what we thought they did when they said what they did. We misinterpret facial expressions, gestures, vocabulary, and terminology. We have to watch this. These are our own imaginations when we think and say, No one loves me, the pastor's against me, or I have no friends. Be careful to cast down the things that you imagine in your mind. Subject every thought to the Word of God. Bring it to the Bible, and make sure that it's a thought produced by God's Spirit, which you can think about legitimately and meditate in. If it isn't a thought from God, cast it out. Otherwise it will just turn into worry, anxiety, and fear, causing you turmoil and opening the door for the sin of familiarity to enter into your heart.

LOOK UNTO JESUS
(Hebrews 12:2)

Look unto Jesus, the Author and Finisher of our faith. Don't look unto the local church, the pastor, the doctrine, or the vision. All these things will fail you in some way. When you look unto Jesus and keep your eyes on Him, everything else is blurred. Your vision of Jesus will remain clear. This will keep you right and allow you to walk in beautiful expectation.

A THANKFUL HEART
(Deuteronomy 28:47-48)

We should serve the Lord with a thankful and joyful heart. Otherwise, we will serve our enemies. I don't know about you, friend, but I don't want to serve any of my enemies, especially not the spiritual ones. I don't want to serve demons or satan or any of his practices or doctrines of demons or any of the religiosity that's in the world today. I want to serve Christ, and Christ alone! I want to serve with my brothers and sisters.

Make sure that you stay joyful and keep your heart full of thanksgiving. Constantly be praying with thanksgiving in your heart, giving thanks and making melody there.

GIVE HONOR WHERE HONOR IS DUE (Romans 13:7)

Give reverence where reverence is due. Be sure to do this, even if it's not due in your personal opinion. If someone deserves to be honored or titled, do it for your own sake. Otherwise, the sin of familiarity may grip you, and it will be your own fault.

ESTEEM LEADERSHIP (1 Thessalonians 5:12-13)

Esteem leadership highly in love for their work's sake. Learn to honor those who are toiling and laboring—for their work's sake. Learn to honor the work of the gospel and the ministry of the Lord Jesus Christ, even if you have a personality conflict or a personal disagreement and even if you've had a confrontation with that person. Still honor them and esteem them very highly in love because of the work's sake, and the Lord will cause you to be at peace.

There's so much more that I could say, but the limited space in this book does not permit further elaboration at this time. Look for more writings on principles that will help you to war a good warfare and to walk with our God in these final days of Church history.

PRAYER OF SALVATION

YOU CAN BE SAVED FROM ETERNAL DAMNATION and get God's help now in this life. All you have to do is humble your heart, believe in Christ's work at Calvary for you, and pray the prayer below.

Dear Heavenly Father,

I know that I have sinned and fallen short of Your expectations of me. I have come to realize that I cannot run my own life. I do not want to continue the way I've been living, neither do I want to face an eternity of torment and damnation.

I know that the wages of sin is death, but I can be spared from this through the gift of the Lord Jesus Christ. I believe that He died for me, and I receive His provision now. I will not be ashamed of Him, and I will tell all my friends and family members that I have made this wonderful decision.

Dear Lord Jesus,

Come into my heart now and live in me and be my Savior, Master, and Lord. I will do my very best to chase after You and to learn Your ways by submitting to a pastor, reading my Bible, going to a church that preaches about You, and keeping sin out of my life.

I also ask You to give me the power to be healed from any sickness and disease and to deliver me from those things that have me bound.

I love You and thank You for having me, and I am eagerly looking forward to a long, beautiful relationship with You.